REAL WORLD DATA

GRAPHING MONEY

Patrick Catel

Chicago, Illinois

www.heinemannraintree.com
Visit our website to find out more information about Heinemann-Raintree books.

To order:
☎ Phone 888-454-2279
▣ Visit www.heinemannraintree.com to browse our catalog and order online.

Edited by Megan Cotugno and Diyan Leake
Designed by Victoria Bevan and Geoff Ward
Original illustrations © Capstone Global Library, LLC 2010
Illustrated by Geoff Ward
Picture research by Ruth Blair, Zooid Pictures Ltd
Originated by Chroma Graphics (Overseas) Pte Ltd
Printed in China by Leo Paper Products Ltd

14 13 12 11 10
10 9 8 7 6 5 4 3 2 1

Library of Congress Cataloging-in-Publication Data

Catel, Patrick.
  Graphing money / Patrick Catel.
    p. cm. -- (Real world data)
  Includes bibliographical references and index.
  ISBN 978-1-4329-2618-2 (hbk.) -- ISBN 978-1-4329-2627-4 (pb) 1. Money--Charts, diagrams, etc.--Juvenile literature. 2. Economics--Charts, diagrams, etc.--Juvenile literature. I. Title.
  HG221.C382 2008
  332.402'1--dc22
                            2009001186

Acknowledgments

The author and publishers are grateful to the following for permission to reproduce copyright material: Alamy p. **4** (© Rob Bartee); Corbis pp. **10** (John and Lisa Merrill), **12** (Wilson Wen/Epa), **14** (Richard Klune); Getty Images pp. **6** (Bill Pierce/Time Life Pictures), **8** (Mpi/Hulton Archive), **18** (Chinafotopress); PA Photos pp. **16** (Richard Drew/Associated Press), **20** (Tomohiro Ohsumi/Pool/Associated Press), **22** (Darron Cummings/Associated Press); Rex Features p. **24**; Shutterstock p. **26** (© Andresr).

Cover photograph of different world currency coins reproduced with permission of Getty Images (Yasuhide Fumoto).

We would like to thank Dr. Michael S. Miller for his invaluable help in the preparation of this book.

Every effort has been made to contact copyright holders of any material reproduced in this book. Any omissions will be rectified in subsequent printings if notice is given to the publisher.

All the Internet addresses (URLs) given in this book were valid at the time of going to press. However, due to the dynamic nature of the Internet, some addresses may have changed, or sites may have changed or ceased to exist since publication. While the author and Publishers regret any inconvenience this may cause readers, no responsibility for any such changes can be accepted by either the author or the Publishers.

CONTENTS

Some words are printed in bold, **like this**. You can find out what they mean by looking in the glossary, on page 30.

MONEY AND ECONOMICS

Human societies have used money in one form or another for centuries. Money is a **medium of exchange** that makes it easier for people to trade with each other. People traded, or bartered, with each other before there was money, but they had to trade one good for another. For example, people might trade apples for clothes. However, the first person may not have clothes to trade. Each trader had to have something the other wanted. It could be very difficult and require several trades to finally get what you wanted.

Money is a special good that everyone is willing to trade for. Once money became a recognized form of exchange, people no longer had to make several trades to get what they needed. Now, they could purchase what they needed as long as they had enough money. The existence of money makes people's lives easier and an economy more efficient. It took people agreeing on what was valuable for money to work. It also took governments guaranteeing the value of their money in order for trade to work internationally.

 Throughout history, people have traded in a variety of types of currency, from beads and cattle to the metal coins shown here.

Economics

Economics is the study of how people choose to use **resources**. Resources include land, buildings, equipment, and other tools. Resources also include time, people, and their ability to produce goods and services. How people choose to use resources includes how much time they spend at work, at school, and having fun; how much money to spend and save; how to use taxes; and the role of government.

The study of economics is broken into two categories: microeconomics and macroeconomics. Microeconomics focuses on the study of how behavior and decisions of an individual person or business affect the economy. It also seeks to understand how people and businesses come to make their economic decisions. Macroeconomics focuses on larger national and international economic trends.

Line graphs

A line graph is a good way to show how data changes over time. Time is always shown on the **x-axis**. The label on the **y-axis** shows the units of measurement. The price of gold in each year is shown as a point (dot). The points are connected to make a line. The line rises up over time, showing that the price of gold is increasing. The steeper the line, the faster the price of gold grows. Gold is a **precious metal** that in the past was used as the **standard** for currency, which was known as the **gold standard**.

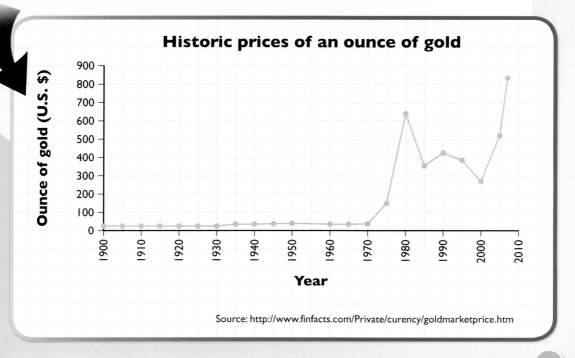

Historic prices of an ounce of gold

Source: http://www.finfacts.com/Private/curency/goldmarketprice.htm

SUPPLY AND DEMAND

The theory of supply and demand is one of the most important concepts of economics. It is also one of the main ideas behind a **market economy**. Supply is how much of something a producer is willing and able to make available for people to buy. Demand is how much of something people want and can afford to buy.

For instance, a local electronics store has 10 new game systems. That is the supply. There are 14 people who want to buy the new game system. That is the demand. Supply and demand are directly linked in a market economy. The goal is to have an equal amount of both in order to have the most efficient economy.

 When many of the oil-producing countries of the world refused to sell oil to the United States in the 1970s, there was clear evidence at gas stations that demand was greater than supply. Drivers lined up and waited for hours to fill up their tanks at the stations that had gasoline.

Price

Price is directly related to supply and demand as well. In fact, price is a way to show the relationship between supply and demand. Usually, the price of something will go up if the demand for that thing goes up. This is because if a lot of people want something (demand), but there is only a limited number of the item (supply), people will be willing to pay more to get the item. The demand goes up. In the same way, the price will usually go down when the demand goes down.

Bar graphs

Like all graphs, bar graphs turn numbers into a picture. This can make them easier to understand. It also helps to show a larger picture, or how things relate to each other. This bar graph shows how many barrels the seven most oil-consuming countries go through each day. You can compare the height of the bars for each country quickly. The United States has the tallest bar and clearly consumes more oil than any other country.

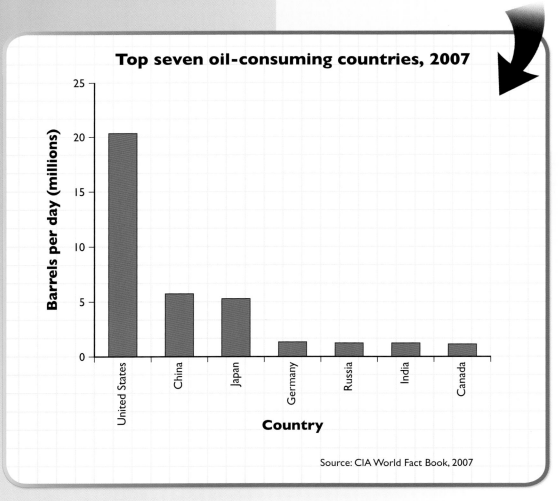

Top seven oil-consuming countries, 2007

Source: CIA World Fact Book, 2007

MONEY AND HISTORY

The desire to trade goods and get rich has been a strong reason for exploration in human history. This was true when the Europeans began exploring other parts of the world. Early explorers came seeking wealth in the form of precious metals and jewels. They often came on behalf of their country, and they often destroyed the **indigenous cultures** they came into contact with.

Later, individuals discovered the land was good for farming and formed **colonies**. Countries and businesses in Europe realized the **raw materials** from the colonies could be shipped back to the mother country. There they could be made into goods to be sold and **exported**. This became part of the idea of trade known as mercantilism.

 Mercantilism led many European powers to want colonies in the New World. However, the practice of mercantilism also made the colonists angry with the mother country. Colonists often paid high prices and taxes on goods that were made from the raw materials they themselves produced.

Mercantilism

Mercantilism is an idea of trade that was followed by major European powers from about 1500 to 1800. It says that a nation should take control of its economy in order to export more than it **imports** and build up gold (money) to make up the difference. The government usually works with private companies to accomplish its aims and uses the money to build a bigger military.

As part of the idea of mercantilism, European powers began to want to develop colonies. A nation could keep its wealth if its colonies provided raw materials to the mother country, and the mother country could sell finished goods to the colonies.

The Great Depression

A stock market is a market for the trading of company **stock** (shares of a company, meaning you own part of the company) at an agreed price. A stock market crash is when there is a sharp drop in share prices of stock listed on the market. Even though, over the long term, the market has gone up in value, there have been famous stock market crashes. The stock market crash of October 24, 1929, became known as Black Thursday. It marked the beginning of the **Great Depression**.

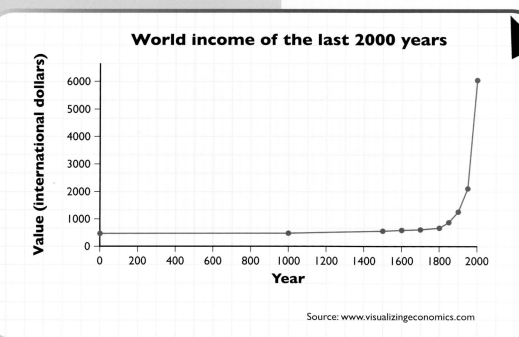

Source: www.visualizingeconomics.com

 This line graph shows that the income level of the world has greatly increased over the last 2,000 years.

FREE ENTERPRISE

A free-enterprise system is one that includes private ownership of property and resources, the ability to make a profit, and the forces of competition and supply and demand to run the market. In a free-enterprise, or capitalist, system, the government usually lets the economy run without too much interference and regulation.

 The free-enterprise system lets people choose what they want to do for a living. It also encourages people to start their own businesses and follow their creative dreams.

Benefits

The free-enterprise system lets people and businesses create, develop, produce, and compete in the marketplace. In this system, no one forces people to do things. People do what they feel is best for them. Since the system is governed by supply and demand, businesses should produce the goods and services that people really need. Therefore this system should lead to the greatest efficiency of any economic system. People also usually think of it as the economic system that is most likely to bring individual freedom and political democracy with it.

What's in a name?

The terms *free enterprise*, *free market*, and **capitalism** are often used to mean basically the same thing. All three of these terms refer to an economic system where private individuals and businesses own the resources and offer goods and services to make money. Government involvement is limited and focuses on protecting a person's right to own property and enforcing **contracts**. The amount of government involvement in a free-market system is different from country to country. How much a government should be involved in a free-market system is a topic that is often debated.

Tables

Tables are another useful way to organize information. When information is set up in tables it is easier to read and understand. This table shows the main parts of a free-enterprise system, the form those parts take, and their role in that system.

The Free-Enterprise System		
Part	**Form of Part**	**Role**
Owners	Private individuals	Individuals own most of the country's resources and decide how to use them.
Organizers	Businesses	Organize resources to produce a good or service efficiently and for a profit.
Brokers	Markets	Bring buyers and sellers together in order for buying and selling to take place.
Protectors	Governments	Protect people's right to own property and enforce voluntary contracts that people enter into.

MASS PRODUCTION

Mass production refers to the manufacture of goods in large quantities. This usually involves the use of designs with interchangeable parts and an **assembly line** for production. Up until the Industrial Revolution, products were made individually by hand. Because of the time, labor, and skill involved, products were expensive and could only be made in limited quantities.

During the Industrial Revolution, there was a change from hand production by home craftspeople to the use of machines and factories. This happened first in England during the late 1700s. The second Industrial Revolution centered on the United States in the mid-1800s.

 Mass production has led to overall improvements in the cost, quality, quantity, and variety of goods available.

Division of labor

By using interchangeable parts, an assembly line, and the idea of **division of labor**, goods can be manufactured in large quantities. Division of labor means that the work required to make something is divided into a number of different tasks that are completed by different workers.

The idea is that when a person only has one specific job to do, the person can become very efficient at that job.

The ideas of mass production have created the largest world economy and population in human history. At the same time, that population, as a whole, also has the highest general **standard of living** in human history.

Comparing data

Multiple bar graphs, like this one, are useful for comparing data quickly. This bar graph shows what percentage of the population of men and women in different countries are employed in the labor force.

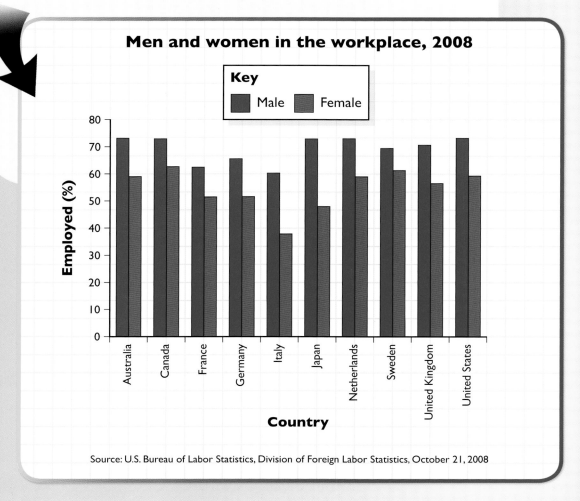

Men and women in the workplace, 2008

Key: Male, Female

Source: U.S. Bureau of Labor Statistics, Division of Foreign Labor Statistics, October 21, 2008

MODERN INDUSTRY

The Industrial Revolution brought the largest economy and population the world has ever seen. The practices of free enterprise and mass production have made many countries and their populations successful. These countries have **developed economies**. However, not all countries of the world are lucky enough to already have modern, industrialized economies. Some countries have developing economies. These are also known as emerging economies.

Countries with developing economies are ones that are not yet fully industrialized. They also usually have a medium to low standard of living. Other factors are considered in how developed a country's economy is. Such factors include per capita income, life expectancy, and the rate of literacy. Per capita income refers to the result when the yearly national income is divided by the population of the country. It is often used to measure the wealth of the population of a country.

Huge amounts of international trade take place every day in the modern world economy.

Economic sectors

In a modern country with a developed economy, there are many sectors, or parts, that make up the economy. The three main economic sectors are agriculture, industry, and services. Agriculture includes any production of goods through growing plants and raising animals. Industry includes all manufacturing, or the making of goods, such as cars or televisions. Services include a wide variety of professions, from truck transportation and warehousing, to health-care services and arts and entertainment.

Pie charts

Pie charts help us to understand **proportion**, which is the size of a group of data compared to other groups. They show the data in different groups as different-sized portions of a circle, like pieces of a pie. In the case of these pie graphs, you can see what proportion each economic sector makes up of each country's economy. You can also compare the makeup of each country's economy by comparing the pie graphs. China's economy, especially, has been booming in recent history.

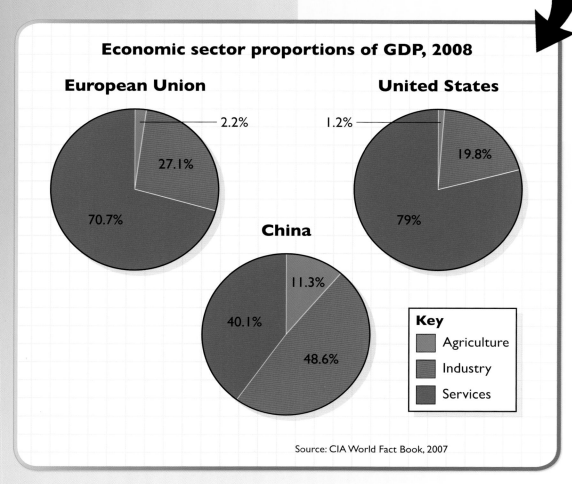

Economic sector proportions of GDP, 2008

European Union

2.2%
27.1%
70.7%

United States

1.2%
19.8%
79%

China

11.3%
40.1%
48.6%

Key
- Agriculture
- Industry
- Services

Source: CIA World Fact Book, 2007

ECONOMIC SYSTEMS

The terms *free enterprise* and *free market* also describe the system of capitalism. In a perfect capitalist, free-market state, the government should not get involved in business and the economy. In reality, however, even in capitalist states the government does have some involvement.

The government of a country usually provides some services, such as the military, education, and certain retirement and health-care benefits. And, it occasionally gets involved in market activity. This situation is known as a mixed economy, because it involves ideas of more than one economic system. The United States has a capitalist mixed economy. This means it is mostly capitalist, but does borrow some ideas from other economic systems.

 A capitalist system, such as in the United States, is a free-market system. People are free to buy and sell shares of companies on the stock market. Wall Street in New York City represents the center of the U.S. stock exchange.

Command economy

Despite the fact that most capitalist countries are actually mixed economies, they are still market economies. This means they will let the market and economy run on its own, with only a little government involvement. The opposite of a market economy is a command economy.

In a command economy, the government controls how things are produced. It also sets the prices of goods and services and makes most of the decisions on how to use resources. Like market economies, command economies often borrow ideas from other economic systems. For this reason, most command economies are also actually mixed economies. They are said to have a command mixed economy. Burma, North Korea, and Cuba are good examples of command economies.

Flow chart

Flow charts are useful tools that make complex systems easier to understand. Sometimes it is easier to show how things are related in a complex system by showing them visually, rather than using a long, written explanation. This flow chart shows how a market economy works.

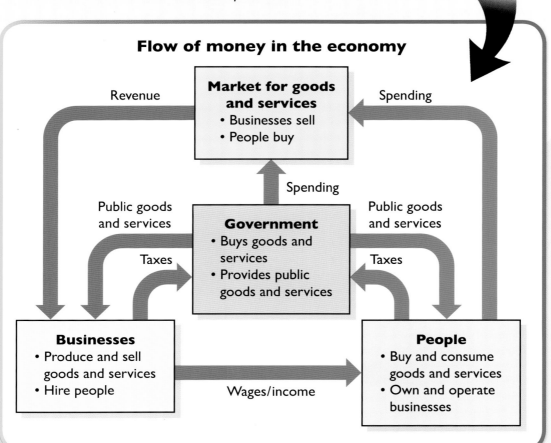

Flow of money in the economy

- **Market for goods and services**
  - Businesses sell
  - People buy
- Revenue
- Spending
- Spending
- Public goods and services
- **Government**
  - Buys goods and services
  - Provides public goods and services
- Public goods and services
- Taxes
- Taxes
- **Businesses**
  - Produce and sell goods and services
  - Hire people
- **People**
  - Buy and consume goods and services
  - Own and operate businesses
- Wages/income

More economic systems

Within the categories of command and market economies, there are even more specific economic systems. Capitalism is one, which we have already explored. Two other economic systems are **socialism** and **communism**.

 China has a command economy. The government has planned and managed its huge economic growth.

Socialism

Socialism is an economic system that believes the state, or its people as a whole, should own and distribute the essential means of production and distribution. Unlike in capitalism, in socialism the motivation of profit is gone from essential industries such as health care and energy. The ideal of socialism is to create a society where everyone has equal wealth. Usually there is a lack of personal freedoms that comes with socialism. Cuba is an example of a socialist state.

Communism

The terms *socialism* and *communism* are often used to mean the same thing. Karl Marx (1818–1883) was a German **philosopher** and **political economist**. He and fellow philosopher Friedrich Engels (1820–1895) published a pamphlet in 1848 called *The Communist Manifesto*. In this work, Marx and Engels explained their ideas of communism to a wide audience.

In the original economic theories of Marx and Engels, socialism is the step that comes after capitalism in the transformation toward communism. According to Marx and Engels, communism is the final stage of economic development of a society. Under communism, there would be a classless society with no state (government). This has not yet happened anywhere in the world, and many socialist states are criticized for the lack of freedoms that their people have.

World economy

This pie chart shows the largest 20 pieces of the world economic pie. The pie chart makes it easy to see which countries have the largest share of the world economy. There are a few countries that stand out as having the largest share: the United States, China, and Japan.

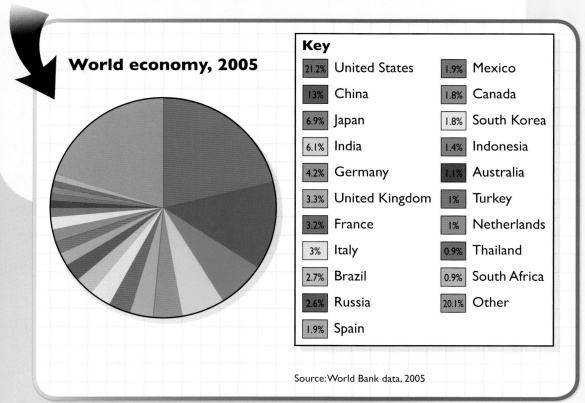

World economy, 2005

Key

21.2%	United States	1.9%	Mexico
13%	China	1.8%	Canada
6.9%	Japan	1.8%	South Korea
6.1%	India	1.4%	Indonesia
4.2%	Germany	1.1%	Australia
3.3%	United Kingdom	1%	Turkey
3.2%	France	1%	Netherlands
3%	Italy	0.9%	Thailand
2.7%	Brazil	0.9%	South Africa
2.6%	Russia	20.1%	Other
1.9%	Spain		

Source: World Bank data, 2005

GROSS DOMESTIC PRODUCT

GDP stands for "gross domestic product." Gross domestic product is the total value of final goods, services, and structures produced within the borders of a country, regardless of the nationality of those who produce them. A United States business operating a plant in Mexico would not have its production added to the U.S. GDP. On the other hand, a Mexican business operating a plant in the United States would have its production added to the U.S. GDP.

The GDP of a country is the figure most often used as a measurement within the world economy. Most countries still measure both their **gross national product** and GDP. And, in most industrialized nations, the two figures are usually very similar.

 With an ever-growing population and better technologies and transportation, the economic world has shrunk. Almost everyone on the planet is now affected by global trade in some way.

Country GDPs

This bar graph is a good way to quickly compare the GDPs of a few countries around the world. Here, the countries were chosen to show different economic systems. Saudi Arabia, Iran, and China all have command economies. The United States, United Kingdom, and Germany have market economies. Chad, Ecuador, and Bangladesh have emerging economies.

The emerging economies of Chad, Ecuador, and Bangladesh are smaller in comparison, as one might expect. As emerging economies, these will likely grow in the years to come. The United States clearly has the highest GDP, with China following. The United States and China have strong, but different, economies. Other factors, such as standard of living (see page 14), would need to be considered in order to see how well off the average American citizen is compared to the average Chinese citizen.

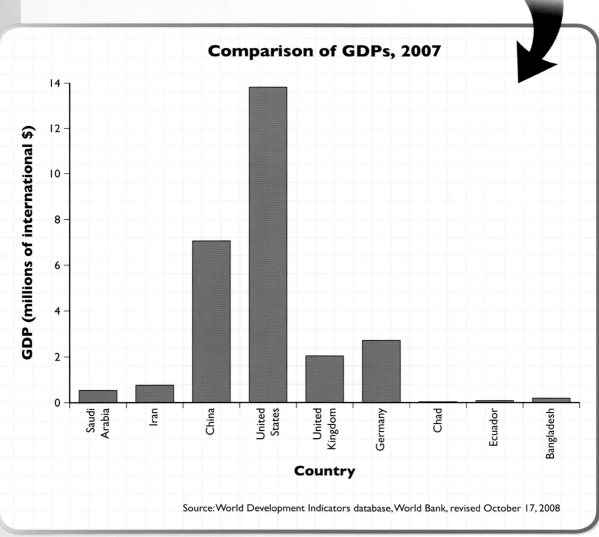

Comparison of GDPs, 2007

Source: World Development Indicators database, World Bank, revised October 17, 2008

GOVERNMENT AND MONEY

Just like a person, household, or business, a government has a budget and must worry about money. Businesses make money by selling goods and services. People make money by working jobs. Governments receive money through **taxes**.

Taxes

A government needs money to defend its people and provide them with services. The way a government gets money is through taxes. Usually both businesses and individual people are taxed. The government uses the taxes it collects to provide public goods and services.

Government goods and services include such things as infrastructure, health care, retirement benefits, education, police and fire services, and national defense. Infrastructure includes things such as roads, bridges, water and sewage treatment, and communication systems.

China's economy has been booming, and they had a budget surplus that allowed them to spend huge amounts of money for the 2008 Summer Olympics.

Debt

A person might take out a loan to buy a house or car. This is called borrowing the money. Usually banks give out loans. When more money is owed than is made, that means the borrower is in debt. Debt is money that is owed to someone else. If a government does not have enough money to pay for all the public goods and services it provides, it too must borrow money.

Usually one government will borrow from another. It then has a debt to the country that loaned it the money. When a country spends more than it takes in during the year, it has a budget **deficit**. The total amount of a government's deficits that it has not yet paid back is its debt. The opposite of a budget deficit is a budget surplus. *Surplus* means "more than enough."

Two y-axes

This bar graph compares the GDPs of ten countries with their unemployment rates. There is a y-axis on each side. The blue bars show the amount in dollars of each country's GDP on the left y-axis. The red bars show the percentage of unemployment on the right y-axis. You can see if there is a relationship between the GDP of a country and its unemployment percentage.

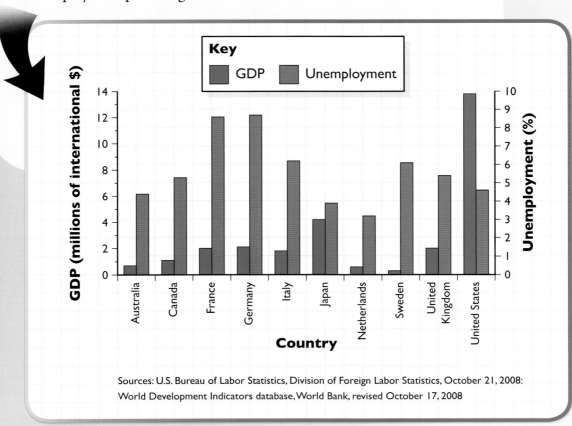

Sources: U.S. Bureau of Labor Statistics, Division of Foreign Labor Statistics, October 21, 2008: World Development Indicators database, World Bank, revised October 17, 2008

Just like businesses and governments, individual people need to make a budget. A good financial goal for an individual might be to have enough money to live, save, and **invest**. It is a good idea to save some money in case you need it for an emergency. By working within a budget, a person will be able to live a more economically secure life.

 It is always a good idea to save money. Banks offer a variety of savings accounts.

Credit or cash?

Today, many people use credit cards to buy goods and services. Many purchases even require a credit card. The popularity of online shopping has also meant an increase in the use of credit cards. When a person uses a credit card, that person is borrowing money to pay for something. The money, plus extra, must be paid back. For these reasons, it is very important to understand how interest rates work.

All credit cards have an APR, which is short for Annual Percentage Rate. *Annual* means "yearly." *Percentage rate* refers to the percentage of interest charged. So, APR refers to the interest charged on a credit card in a year. For instance, if a credit card has an APR of 15%, a balance of $500 would accumulate $75 in a year's time. So the balance would be $575 at the end of a year, if it is not paid off earlier.

Savings

Interest rates can also be good for people. For instance, savings accounts usually have an APR. This means that money put in a savings account will earn interest over time. For instance, $500 left in a savings account at 2% interest (APR) would become $510 after a year.

Multiple line graphs

More than one line graph can be drawn on the same axes. This makes them easier to compare. This graph shows us what would happen to $500 owed to a credit card, or put in a savings account, over seven years if left alone at a constant interest rate. It is clear that the person would benefit most by first paying off the credit card debt.

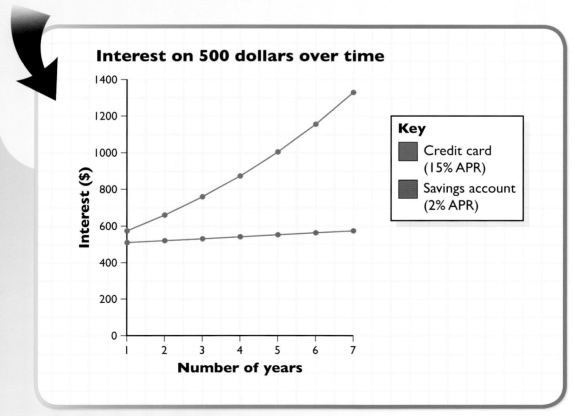

Investing

A person can also invest part of the money they have saved. When people invest part of their savings, they are putting that money at risk and hoping to make more money more quickly. An investment is owning something or a part of something the owner hopes will gain money. Stocks (shares of businesses) are an example of this. There is always a risk that the money invested could be lost. However, some investments are riskier than others, and some likely to make more money than others. It is important to make an educated decision when investing money.

 It is generally true that the higher your education, the more money you will likely make in your lifetime.

Why should I study?

Saving money is important. Understanding how credit cards and interest rates work is also important. Having economic knowledge is essential for life in the modern world. However, a good education in general has been proven to pay off.

If you study hard and get a good education, it really can pay. For instance, in 2007, a person with a Master's degree earned $561 more per week than a high-school graduate. In their lifetimes, the high-school graduate might earn $1.2 million, and the person with the Master's degree might earn $2.5 million. That's double the income of a high-school graduate over the course of a lifetime. Remember how valuable an education is the next time you feel like you don't want to be at school!

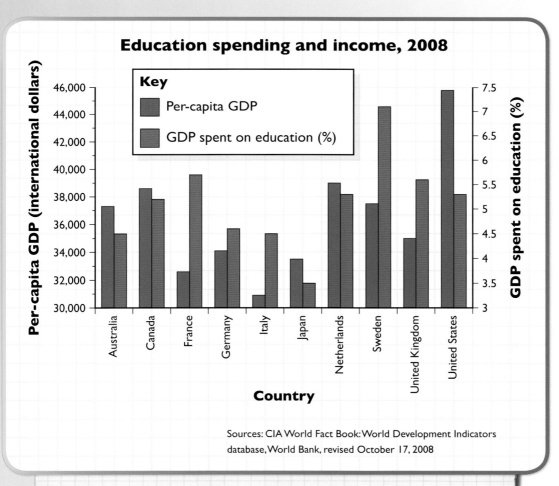

Education spending and income, 2008

Per-capita GDP (international dollars) — left axis: 30,000; 32,000; 34,000; 36,000; 38,000; 40,000; 42,000; 44,000; 46,000

GDP spent on education (%) — right axis: 3; 3.5; 4; 4.5; 5; 5.5; 6; 6.5; 7; 7.5

Key
- Per-capita GDP
- GDP spent on education (%)

Countries: Australia, Canada, France, Germany, Italy, Japan, Netherlands, Sweden, United Kingdom, United States

Country

Sources: CIA World Fact Book: World Development Indicators database, World Bank, revised October 17, 2008

This bar graph shows per-capita GDP, which roughly shows how much money a person in the country might make in year's time. It also shows what percent of the GDP each country spends on education.

Data is information about something. We often get important data as a mass of numbers, and it is difficult to make any sense of them. Graphs and charts are ways of displaying information visually. This helps us to see relationships and patterns in the data. Different types of graphs or charts are good for displaying different types of information.

Pie charts

Pie charts show information as different-sized portions of a circle. They can help you compare proportions. The whole circle shows the whole of the data. A large sector (piece of pie) means that a large proportion of data is in that group.

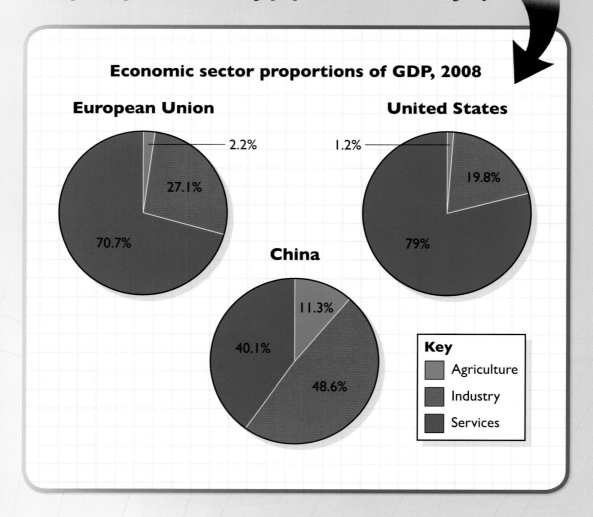

Economic sector proportions of GDP, 2008

European Union

2.2%

27.1%

70.7%

United States

1.2%

19.8%

79%

China

11.3%

40.1%

48.6%

Key
Agriculture
Industry
Services

Line graphs

Line graphs use lines to connect points on a graph. They can be used to show how data changes over time. Time is always shown on the x-axis. More than one line graph can be drawn on the same axes.

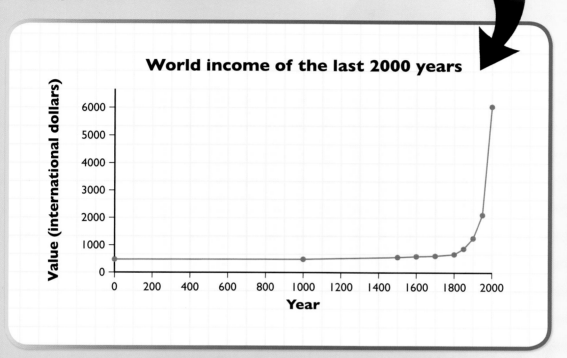

Bar graphs

Bar graphs are a good way to compare the results of a survey or an investigation. Bar graphs have a y-axis showing **frequency** and an x-axis showing the different types of information. When you are drawing graphs, always label each axis and give your graph a title.

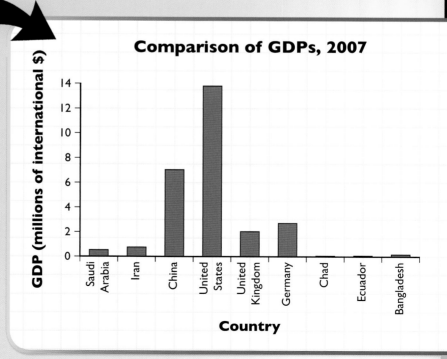

GLOSSARY

assembly line arrangement of workers and machines where the product being assembled passes from one stage to another until finished

capitalism economic system in which the means of production are owned by individuals or corporations, not the government

colony new territory, and the people living in it, which still has ties to a parent state, or mother country

communism economic system where all the people own all the property, together, and labor is organized for the benefit of everyone

contract agreement between two or more parties for doing something, often enforced by law

currency money or something else that is used as a medium of exchange

deficit amount by which a sum of money is too small

developed economy economy that is industrialized

division of labor dividing a job into parts where a worker or group is assigned to each part. It is part of mass production and allows more of something to be produced.

export send something to another country for sale or exchange

frequency number of things in a group of data

gold standard agreement by countries to fix the value of their currencies based on a specific amount of gold.

Great Depression economic crisis and period of low business activity in the U.S. and other countries. It started with the stock market crash in October 1929 and lasted most of the 1930s.

gross national product total value of goods and services produced by the residents of a country, even if they work outside the country

import bring something into a country from another country for sale or exchange

indigenous culture group of people or way of life originating in or native to a particular region or country

invest using money to purchase something (an investment) which, in time, may give more money in return, as interest or an increase in value

market economy involves the private ownership of the means of production (for example, farms and factories), with supply and demand determining the price of goods and use of resources

medium of exchange something accepted in exchange for goods and services and recognized as having a standard, known value

philosopher person who offers views and theories on difficult questions to do with philosophy and logic, and who may establish the central ideas of a way of thinking

political economist person involved in the study of political policies, economic processes, and their influence on society

precious metal one that is less common and has high economic value, such as gold, platinum, and silver

proportion size of one group of data compared to the whole set of data or to other groups

raw material material before being processed or manufactured; for instance, cotton is a raw material used to make clothing

resource something that can be used, often to make money; factories, labor (workers), and raw materials are all resources

socialism economic system based on the state ownership of industry, where a central body or government plans and controls essential sectors of the economy

standard something used as a point of comparison, approved by people in general or an authority or government

standard of living level of material comfort, or goods and services, that a person has

stock share, or small part, of a company or business

tax sum of money charged by a government for its support and for public services it provides

x-axis horizontal line on a graph

y-axis vertical line on a graph

FURTHER INFORMATION

Books

Bochner, Arthur, and Rose Bochner. *The New Totally Awesome Money Book for Kids, Revised and Updated Edition*. New York: Newmarket Press, 2007.

Challen, Paul. *What Is Supply and Demand? [Economics in Action]*. New York: Crabtree Publishing, 2009.

Cribb, Joe. *Money [DK Eyewitness Books]*. New York: DK Publishing, 2005.

Gilman, Laura Anne. *Economics [How Economics Works]*. Minneapolis, Minn.: Lerner Publications, 2005.

Harman, Hollis Page. *Money Sense for Kids*. Hauppauge, NY: Barron's Educational Books, 2005.

Websites

This U.S. government website helps teach the basics in financial education. There are many resources to help people make wise financial decisions. www.mymoney.gov

This website is a virtual community designed to entertain and educate players, teaching the concept of a market and the basics of economics. www.Minyanland.com

This site provides resources for students, teachers, and parents on how to manage money and develop good financial habits. www.themint.org

This is the site of the most recent Economic Census of the U.S. Census Bureau. Here you can find many statistics concerning the U.S. economy. www.census.gov/econ/census07/index.html

INDEX